The Sun
in Me

Poems About the Planet

For Joyce and Harry, with love — J. N.
For my father, who is like sunshine — B. K.

Barefoot Books
2067 Massachusetts Ave
Cambridge, MA 02140

First published in the United States of America in 2003 by Barefoot Books, Inc.
This paperback edition published in 2008

This book has been printed on 100% acid-free paper
Graphic design by Applecart, England. Color separation by Grafiscan, Verona
Printed and bound in Singapore by Tien Wah Press Pte Ltd
This book was typeset in Optima and Friz Quadrata
The illustrations were prepared using scratchboard and watercolor

Paperback ISBN 978-1-84686-161-1

The Library of Congress cataloged the hardcover edition as follows:
The sun in me : poems about the planet / [edited by] Judith Nicholls, Beth Krommes.
    p. cm.
  ISBN 1-84148-058-4 (hardcover : alk. paper)
  1. Nature--Juvenile poetry. I. Nicholls, Judith. II. Krommes, Beth, ill.
  PN6110.N2S78 2003
  808.81'936--dc22

                          2005022747

          1 3 5 7 9 8 6 4 2

The Sun in Me

Poems About the Planet

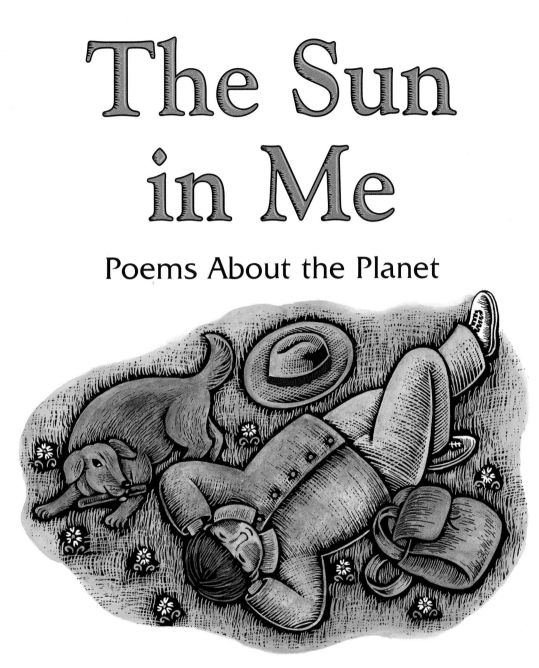

compiled by **Judith Nicholls**

illustrated by **Beth Krommes**

Barefoot Books
Celebrating Art and Story

Contents

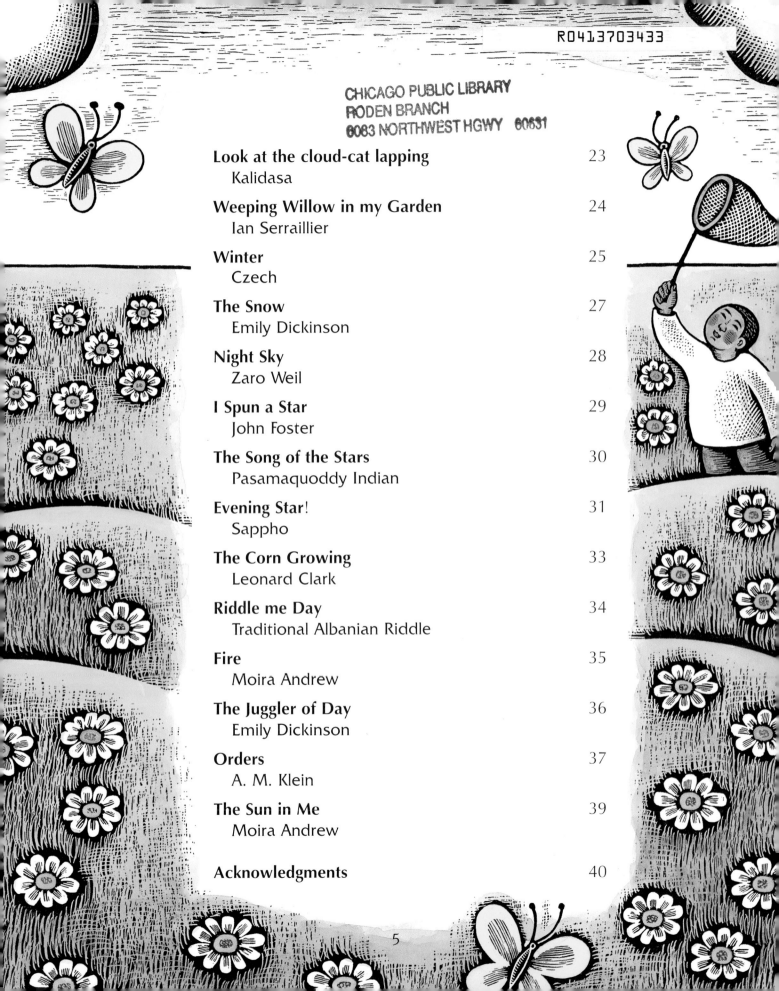

INTRODUCTION

What could be more beautiful than a blazing sunrise, a star-filled sky, or a thick, leafy forest that stretches as far as the eye can see? How can we, as human beings, begin to represent these images of nature in a way that captures their magic and mystery? For centuries, poets and artists all around the world have struggled to do just this — to represent the sights and sounds of nature, and the feelings that nature evokes in us. What strikes me about these poems is that each of the poets, in their very different ways, has somehow succeeded in capturing some of those qualities on the page.

Though nature can be a destructive force at times, each poem here celebrates it in some way. Mary Kawena Pukui's poem reminds us that some aspects of nature — flowers, birds, trees, fish — are found the world over, providing a shared experience and vocabulary across many cultures. Her use of repetition helps transmit some of the joy she felt when surrounded by the beauty of her native Hawaii: her poem almost begs to be shouted from a mountain top! Canadian poet A. M. Klein's quietly contrasting poem *Orders* is no less celebratory about the sense of peace nature can inspire: "Let me sit silent,/ Let me wonder."

Japanese poets, like their artists, often capture whole worlds in the simplest of brush-strokes: Issa paints a picture of wind and mountain in a five-word haiku and Buson's wonderful eight-word eulogy radiates with the awe that the moon can inspire. John Updike also reveals the many identities of his *Winter Ocean* with arresting precision. "Many-maned scud-thumper," "sky-mocker" and "wind-slave" suggest perfectly the complex mystery of the ocean. Equally remarkable is the simple but broad-sweeping image at the end of Leonard Clark's poem, *The*

Corn Growing. In just three words he manages to incorporate all the spirit-raising mystery of growth and rebirth in the natural world.

Many of the poems not only encourage the celebration of nature, but also ask us to respect and conserve the natural wilderness we have. David McCord suggests that we look, listen and "let be," rather than continually try to impose on it our own human presence. Grace Nichols, too, begs us to respect the majesty of the forest in her powerful last lines: "Forest could keep secrets/ And we must keep Forest."

Most of all, these poems show us what it is to see nature through eyes of wonder and curiosity, as a child might see it. Nature, through a poet's eyes, is both seen in a new light, then transformed into a new shape — a poem — through the medium of words. Emily Dickinson, one of my favorite, most admired poets, is able to do this time and time again. What other word-artist could describe the sunset with such fresh, powerful imagery? "Blazing in Gold and quenching in Purple/ Leaping like Leopards to the Sky..."

As a part of nature, we all have the ability to appreciate it, to celebrate and to respect it, and to find it within ourselves. "Sing out and say/ Again the refrain/ Behold this lovely world," pleads Mary Kawena Pukui. I hope that through these poems you will enjoy sharing and celebrating our beautiful world with the children in your care and that they will indeed be open to the sun in each of them.

Judith Nicholls

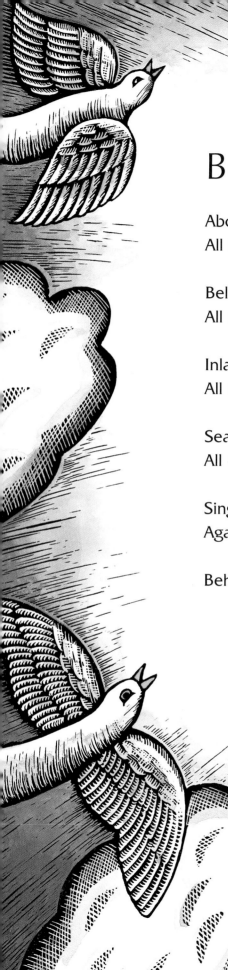

Behold

Above, above
All birds in air

Below, below
All earth's flowers

Inland, inland
All forest trees

Seaward, seaward
All ocean fish

Sing out and say
Again the refrain

Behold this lovely world

Mary Kawena Pukui

Look!

Look at the sunlight
shaking patterns
through the trees

Look at the raindrops
cupped cool green
in cassava leaves

Look at the bananas
turning
nice and fat and ripe

Look at the watermelon —
how about
a sweet mouth-watering red slice

Grace Nichols

Father and I in the Woods

"Son,"
My father used to say,
"Don't run."

"Walk,"
My father used to say,
"Don't talk."

"Words,"
My father used to say,
"Scare birds."

So be:
It's sky and brook and bird
And tree.

David McCord

The shy speechless sound

The shy speechless sound
of a fruit falling from its tree,
and around it the silent music
of the forest, unbroken...

Osip Mandelstam
Translated by Clarence Brown

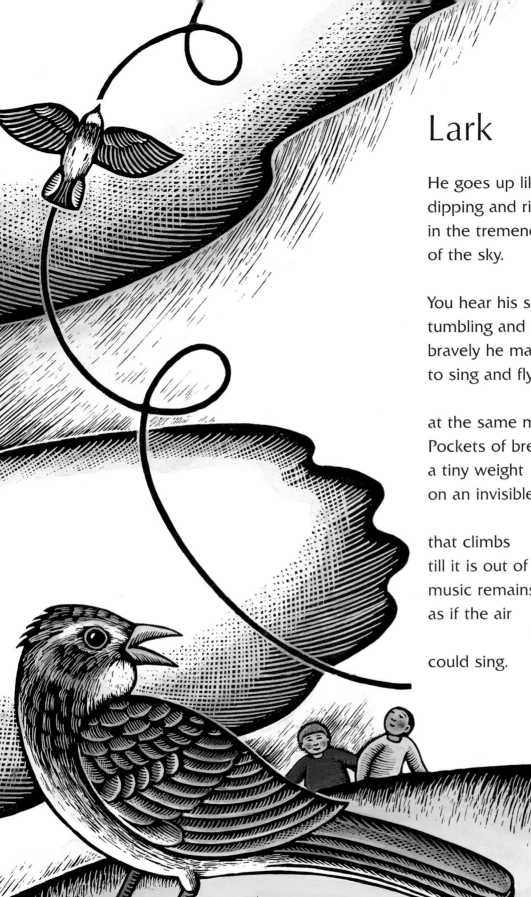

Lark

He goes up like a yo-yo
dipping and rising
in the tremendous distance
of the sky.

You hear his song, first,
tumbling and ecstatic…
bravely he manages
to sing and fly

at the same moment.
Pockets of breath sustain him —
a tiny weight
on an invisible string

that climbs
till it is out of sight, and only
music remains —
as if the air

could sing.

Jean Kenward

13

For Forest

Forest could keep secrets
Forest could keep secrets

Forest tune in every day
to watersound and birdsound
Forest letting her hair down
to the teeming creeping of her forest-ground

But Forest don't broadcast her business
no Forest cover her business down
from sky and fast-eye sun
and when night come
and darkness wrap her like a gown
Forest is a bad dream woman

Forest dreaming about mountain
and when earth was young
Forest dreaming of the caress of gold
Forest rootsing with mysterious Eldorado

and when howler monkey
wake her up with howl
Forest just stretch and stir
to a new day of sound

but coming back to secrets
Forest could keep secrets
Forest could keep secrets

And we must keep Forest

Grace Nichols

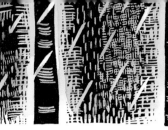

Everything's Wet

Everything's wet
in the woods today,
hung with a silver chain.
All night long
came the slushing sound
of calling
      falling
           rain.

I heard it as
I went to sleep.
I heard it when I fell
into a dreamful nothingness —
and when I woke,
as well.

Jean Kenward

Horse of the Sea

I'll mount my ocean steed
And over the hills I'll speed.
Forests and hills are not for me
I love the moving sea.

Snorri Sturlason
Translated by S. Laing

Winter Ocean

Many-maned scud-thumper, tub
of male whales, maker of worn wood, shrub-
ruster, sky-mocker, rave!
portly pusher of waves, wind-slave.

John Updike

from Stray Birds

"What language is thine, O sea?"
　　"The language of eternal question."
"What language is thy answer, O sky?"
　　"The language of eternal silence."

Rabindranath Tagore

River Winding

Rain falling, what things do you grow?
Snow melting, where do you go?
Wind blowing, what trees do you know?
River winding, where do you flow?

Charlotte Zolotow

Haiku

Rain drums on the pane
and runs down, wavering the world
into a dream

J. W. Hackett

Autumn wind —
    mountain's shadow
      wavers.

Issa
Translated by Lucien Stryk
and Takashi Ikemoto

Is it a shower of rain?
I thought as I listened
From my bed, just awake.
But it was falling leaves
Which could not stand the wind.

Priest Saigyo
Translated by Geoffrey Bownas and
Anthony Thwaite

Such a moon —
the thief
pauses to sing.

Buson

Translated by Lucien Stryk and Takashi Ikemoto

Look at the cloud-cat lapping there on high
With lightening tongue the moon-milk
from the sky!

Kalidasa

Weeping Willow in my Garden

My willow's like a frozen hill
Of green waves, when the wind is still
But when it blows, the waves unfreeze
And make a waterfall of leaves.

Ian Serraillier

Winter

In the night,
Came a white horse to visit,
His hooves made no sound
As he covered the ground,
And snow filled the land with its spirit.

Czech
Translated by Andrew Fusek Peters

The Snow

It sifts from Leaden Sieves —
It powders all the Wood.
It fills with Alabaster Wool
The Wrinkles of the Road —

It makes an Even Face
Of Mountain, and of Plain —
Unbroken Forehead from the East
Unto the East again —

It reaches to the Fence —
It wraps it Rail by Rail
Till it is lost in Fleeces —
It deals Celestial Vail

To Stump, and Stack — and Stem —
A Summer's empty Room —
Acres of Joints, where Harvests were,
Recordless, but for them —

It Ruffles Wrists of Posts
As Ankles of a Queen —
Then stills its Artisans — like Ghosts —
Denying they have been —

Emily Dickinson

Night Sky

Night sky
Floods my room
Oh
My heart pounds
The moon is
Now my own.

Zaro Weil

I Spun a Star

I spun a star
Which gleamed and glittered in the night.
I spun a star,
Stood watching spellbound from afar,
Until it disappeared from sight,
A shimmering speck of silver light.
I spun a star.

John Foster

The Song of the Stars

We are the stars which sing.
We sing with our light.
We are the birds of fire
We fly across the heaven.

from a Pasamaquoddy Indian song

Evening Star!

Evening star! You bring back
All that the bright dawn scattered;
You bring back the sheep to the fold
That wandered all day on the hillside.
You bring back the goat, and you bring
The child back home to its mother.

Sappho
Translated by Beram Saklatvala

The Corn Growing

Snow no longer snowing,
Wind ends its blowing,
Every stream fresh flowing,
A cockerel loudly crowing,
New grass blades slowly showing,
A bullock deeply lowing,
The chilly evenings going,
And almost without knowing,
The corn growing.

Leonard Clark

Riddle me Day

It rolls over rock, and never gets torn
It runs through the bush untouched by the thorn
It falls into water, but cannot sink down
It dives in the sea, yet cannot drown.

Traditional Albanian Riddle
Translated by Elona Velca and
Andrew Fusek Peters

Fire

Fire lives in the heart
of a summer poppy,
 spills blood-red
from the rising sun.

Fire winks its eye
from the geranium,
 dreams of flame
all the long afternoon.

Fire sleeps in the
dark of a night rose,
 slumbers ash-cold
in the pale moonlight.

Moira Andrew

The Juggler of Day

Blazing in Gold and quenching in Purple
Leaping like Leopards to the Sky
Then at the feet of the old Horizon
Laying her spotted Face to die
Stooping as low as the Otter's Window
Touching the Roof and tinting the Barn
Kissing her Bonnet to the Meadow
And the Juggler of Day is gone

Emily Dickinson

Orders

Muffle the wind;
Silence the clock;
Muzzle the mice;
Curb the small talk;
Cure the hinge-squeak;
Banish the thunder.
Let me sit silent,
Let me wonder.

A. M. Klein

The Sun in Me

The sun is in me,
pale morning flames
setting my still-sleeping
         heart alight.

The wind is in me,
clear blue breath
leading my bare feet
         into a new day.

The sea is in me,
deep green waves
whispering wild music
         in my ears.

The river is in me,
dark brown waters
swirling its questions
         around my head.

The moon is in me,
sad silver beams
painting my dreams
         with shadows.

Moira Andrew

ACKNOWLEDGEMENTS

"Behold" by Mary Kawena Pukui, copyright © Mary Kawena Pukui, from *The Penguin Book of Oral Poetry*. "Look!" by Grace Nichols, copyright © Grace Nichols. "Father and I in the Woods" by David McCord, copyright © David McCord, from *Few and Far Between,* published by Little, Brown and Co. "The shy speechless sound" by Osip Mandelstam, English translation copyright © Clarence Brown and W.S. Merwin 1973, reprinted from *Selected Poems* by permission of Oxford University Press. "Lark" by Jean Kenward, copyright © Jean Kenward. "For Forest" by Grace Nichols, copyright © Grace Nichols. "Everything's Wet" by Jean Kenward, copyright © Jean Kenward. "Winter Ocean" by John Updike, copyright © John Updike, from *Telegraph Poles*, published by André Deutsch Ltd. "River Winding" by Charlotte Zolotow, copyright © Charlotte Zolotow. "Rain drums on the pane," J. W. Hackett from *Junior Voices*, ed. Geoffrey Summerfield, published by Penguin Books. "Autumn wind" by Issa, translated by Lucien Stryk and Takashi Ikemoto, from *The Penguin Book of Zen Poetry*, published by Penguin Books. "Is it a shower of rain?" by Priest Saigyo, translated by Geoffrey Brownas and Anthony Thwaite, from *The Penguin Book of Zen Poetry*, published by Penguin Books. "Such a moon" by Buson from *The Penguin Book of Zen Poetry,* published by Penguin Books. "Look at the cloud-cat lapping" by Kalidasa, theme epigraphs from *Poems from the Sanskrit*, translated by J. Brough (Penguin Classics 1968), copyright © John Brough 1968, reprinted by permission of Penguin Books Ltd. "Weeping Willow in my Garden" by Ian Seraillier from *I'll Tell You A Tale*, published by Puffin Books, 1976. "Winter" translated by Andrew Fusek Peters. "The Snow" by Emily Dickinson, reprinted by permission of the publishers and the Trustees of Amherst College from *The Poems of Emily Dickinson*, Thomas H. Johnson, ed., Cambridge, Mass.: The Belknap Press of Harvard University Press, Copyright © 1951, 1955, 1979 by the president and Fellows of Harvard College. "Night Sky" by Zaro Weil, from *Mud, Moon and Me*, first published in the UK by Orchard Books in 1989, a division of the The Watts Publishing Group Limited, 96 Leonard Street, London EC2A 4XD. "I Spun a Star" by John Foster, copyright © John Foster, from *Climb Aboard the Poetry Plane* (Oxford University Press), included by permission of the author. "Evening Star" by Sappho, translated by Beram Saklatvala, reprinted with permission of Charles Skilton/Caversham Communications. "The Corn Growing" by Leonard Clark, copyright © Leonard Clark, from *The Corn Growing* published by Hodder & Stoughton, 1982. "Riddle me Day" translated by Andrew Fusek Peters and Elona Velca. "Fire" by Moira Andrew, copyright © Moira Andrew, 2003. "The Juggler of Day" by Emily Dickinson, reprinted by permission of the publishers and the Trustees of Amherst College from *The Poems of Emily Dickinson*, Thomas H. Johnson, ed., Cambridge, Mass.: The Belknap Press of Harvard University Press, Copyright © 1951, 1955, 1979 by the president and Fellows of Harvard College. "Orders" by A. M. Klein, from *The New Wind Has Wings*, poems from Canada, comp. Mary Alice Downie and Barbara Robertson, Oxford University Press Toronto/Oxford, 1984. "The Sun in Me" by Moira Andrew, copyright © Moira Andrew, first published in *I'm in a Mood Today*, edited by John Foster (Oxford University Press).

The publishers have made every effort to contact holders of copyright material. If you have not received our correspondence, please contact us for inclusion in future editions.